BIRMINGHAM'S FIRST BLACK POLICEMAN: AN INSPIRATIONAL STORY

A THREE DECADE PERSPECTIVE

Bessie Stover Powell, Ed. D.

Don Lance Powell, Ph. D.

Leroy Stover, B.S., Deputy Chief

"with God all things are Possible"

Deputy Chief Leroy Stoner

DEDICATIONS

This book is dedicated to my uncle, Leroy, above all, who paved the way for many others to follow in the Birmingham Areas and the Police Department. As his oldest niece, I am blessed and honored to have him in our family. He is courageous, a risk taker, a role model, and an inspiration for many. I believe that his *life mission, a Moses type mission, was* to lead the way for generations of Blacks previously denied access to the law enforcement profession, before March 30, 1966.

This book is also In memory of my grandparents, Mose and Bessie Stover (uncle Leroy's parents), who helped raise me and Dr. James Wallace, my cousin, who is more like a brother. They taught us to work hard and have Christian values. To my mother, Georgia, Aunt Josephine, Uncle Norman and Albert, all of Uncle Leroy's living siblings, I honor and adore you. Uncle Moses Jr.

and Robert are Uncle Leroy's deceased brothers who also helped to influence and shape his life.

To my family, friends, colleagues, students and grand-children (Vania, JaiDon, Jerrae, Miniya, Brannon Joel, Morgan, Adonis, and Raigon) always be cognizant that one person's courage can affect a life, city, state, nation and the world.

This book is also dedicated to the second Black Policeman hired, Chief Johnnie Johnson. The third Black Policeman Robert Boswell is also acknowledged for his historical significance. We also honor the thousands of people who marched, volunteered and sacrificed their lives so that doors and opportunities could be opened where they were denied. All of your labor is not in vain. We are standing on your shoulders.

OUR OLDEST SON, WHO LOVED UNCLE LEROY, (whose relationship became closer while attending Miles College and who completed South Carolina State University with a B.S. in Criminal Justice, May 1994)

Don Lance Powell, Jr.

07-04-70 TO 09 -14 -1996

TABLE OF CONTENTS

I. THE EARLY YEARS: THE FOUNDATION-
   SELMA/SARDIS ALABAMA 15
   A. HIGH SCHOOL- SHILOH HIGH
      SCHOOL
   B. MILITARY -82ND AIRBORNE DIVISION,
      FT. BRAGG, NC. 187th AIRBORNE
      REGIMENTAL COMBAT TEAM-
      KOREA/JAPAN
   C. TRANSITIONING
   D. PERSONAL RECOLLECTIONS

II. BIRMINGHAM TRIUMPH- THE BEGINNING. . 29

   A. SETTING– FIRST 10 YEARS 1966 -1976
   B. HISTORICAL DOCUMENTS
   C. CHALLENGES AND ACCOMPLISHMENTS
   D. PERSONAL RECOLLECTIONS

III. SECOND DECADE 56

   A. SETTING – 1977 – 1987
   B. HISTORICAL DOCUMENTS

C. CHALLENGES AND ACCOMPLISHMENTS

D. PERSONAL RECOLLECTIONS

IV. THIRD DECADE 71

A. SETTING 1988 – 1998

B. HISTORICAL DOCUMENTS

C. CHALLENGES AND ACCOMPLISHMENTS

D. PERSONAL RECOLLECTIONS

V. FAMILY REFLECTIONS 98

VI. SUMMARY 118

VII. BIBLIOGRAPHY 123

PREFACE

Don L. Powell, B.A., M.A., Ph. D.

It is not often that the person who inspires you lives around the corner or right across the street. However, this was the case for me as a young African- American male growing up in one of the most segregated cities, not only in the south, but in America, Birmingham, Alabama. It later became infamously known as" bombing-ham" because of the racially inspired bombings that resulted in the deaths of four young inno-cent Black girls, on a Sunday morning, at the 16th Street Baptist Church, in the city. This was one of the most tragic events of the growing civil rights movement and caused its leader, Dr. Martin Luther King Jr., to target Birmingham as one of the most segregated cities in the coun-try. It was against this racially oppressive back-drop that Leroy Stover emerged as the first Black Policeman to be hired by the City of Birmingham on March 30, 1966. When this happened in the city of arch-segregationist, Eugene "Bull" Conner, it was a major news story, in the papers and on television, in many areas of the country. Always intellectually curious and socially conscious I stayed attuned to as much as possible.

I lived in Englewood, the same small all-Black community as Deputy Chief Stover, who had migrated there with his family from the cotton fields of Sardis, Alabama. I graduated from Fairfield Industrial High School (a suburb of Birmingham) in 1963, three years prior to Deputy Chief Stover assuming his position. My high school years were uniquely formative for me because I was diligently searching for a positive Black male role model that I knew and could identify with. This is a dire social need for many young Black males, even today, and in the segregated 60's in Birmingham, Alabama, there was an even greater need for successful Black male role models. The newly chosen first Black Policeman, Leroy Stover, became this inspiring symbol for me.

My family and I lived one street over from Deputy Chief Stover and his family. Eventually we moved across the street from them in Englewood. Being in such close proximity, I saw him nearly everyday (I later married his niece, Bessie). The first example that my uncle provided me was that of a Black man being impeccably dressed in his starched and ironed police uniform, with his policeman's hat and shiny badge, and a gun on his side. No other Black man I knew could lawfully dress like this or carry such a weapon of authority.

As I saw Deputy Chief Stover go and come over the years, driving his police car in and out of the Englewood Community, his demeanor and behavior never changed. He was never boastful and always courteous with a smile and hearty laughter as he is to this day. As I reflect on it, I am sure that he never knew the tremendous impact that he had on me growing up. He was a black man who had pride and dignity, who was not afraid in a racially charged atmosphere and who met all the qualifications to become Birmingham's first Black Policeman. So when I read newspaper articles about Uncle Leroy, or saw him on television, as my elementary school principal would say "it made my chest stick out". This was even more the case, when I saw him directing baseball crowds at Rickwood Field (where the Birmingham Black and White Barons played Baseball). I would often catch the local #5 bus to go to these games. Uncle Leroy could also be seen directing large crowds at the Fairgrounds at Five Points West in Birmingham. His police authority also extended to (Ensley) West Precinct as well as the North Precinct (downtown, North Birmingham and Cottageville areas around the city of Birmingham). Many African American citizens and others, throughout the Birmingham area, and eventually the state of Alabama, came to know, love, and respect Deputy Chief Stover.

A parent tree puts out many branches. Deputy Chief Stover has been an exemplary and noble role model for other African Americans to follow, when it comes to filling the ranks of the Birmingham Police. For me, he has been a constant source of inspiration, and a sterling example that pulling yourself up by your own bootstraps is still possible for those who persevere against the odds. I am very proud of Deputy Chief Stover and to call him my family member. He has earned his place in history.

Acknowledgements

I express my gratitude to family, friends, colleagues and students for their interest and encouragement. I especially thank the following individuals (all educators), for their expertise and assistance:

> Don Lance Powell, Ph.D. (Husband)-Co-Editor, *Voorhees College*
>
> Brannon J. Powell, ABD, (Son) - Contributing Writer
>
> Minita Powell Clark, Ed. S. (Daughter) - Contributing Writer, *Benedict College*
>
> Joi Powell Wade, M. Ed., (Daughter) - Manuscript Reviewer, *Whittaker Elementary School, Orangeburg School District 5*

Special honor and gratefulness goes to my Uncle Leroy for trusting me to tell his story, with his assistance. I also thank Aunt Joe Ann Stover for assisting with the historical data collection. I always told him, *"one day I will write your*

story". I thank my publishers. They have been a blessing to me, for their support and guidance in this process.

Part I

The Early Years: The Foundation
(Selma/Sardis, Alabama)

Bessie Stover Powell, B.S., M.A., Ed D.

The Early Years of Uncle Leroy I remember very well. You see, he was slender, tall, articulate, athletic, handsome and very intelligent. The young ladies would always ask me about him; therefore, I concluded that he was very popular. He is the fifth child of Mose and Bessie Smiley Stover. As the first grandchild, I was named Bessie after my grandmother, Uncle Leroy's mom. He, along with all the Stover siblings, was born in Berlin, Alabama (Sardis, Alabama) about twenty to twenty - two miles south of Selma, Alabama.

As far as I remember, our household consisted of My grandmother, her three youngest sons, Leroy, Norman and Albert, along with the first two grandchildren, my first cousin, James, and me. Grandma and my three uncles had to sharecrop the fields for our living. My grandfather Mose, my mother Georgia, aunt Josephine (James's mother) and older uncles, Robert and Mose Jr., had left rural Sardis for better opportunity for work and school in Fairfield, Alabama. My grandfather, along with Moses Jr., worked at the United States

Steel Plant, Fairfield, Alabama. Uncle Robert went

Leroy and Robert Stover

into the Army but also worked at the Steel Plant until he was laid off, then he reentered the United States Army and retired from Fort Benning, Columbus, Ga. He died on Christmas Day, 2009. He is buried on the Ft. Benning Military Base. It looks

Georgia, Leroy, Josephine, (sisters and Dad) Moses Sr.

just like a miniature version of Arlington Cemetery

in the Washington, D. C. area. Uncle Leroy's two sisters, Georgia (my mother) and Aunt Josephine, retired from the Nursing profession with nearly one-hundred years in health care. Georgia, a Licensed Practical Nurse, completed an Associate Degree, and retired from two health care facilities, with over sixty years total in the profession. Josephine, a Licensed Practical Nurse for four-teen years, later became a Registered Nurse, completed an Associate Degree in Nursing, and retired from a Birmingham hospital with at least thirty-eight years in the profession. Leroy's sister,

Leroy and Dad

Georgia, the oldest sibling, cared for the younger children, baby sat, cooked, cleaned house as well as worked in the field. Josephine, the youngest sister, born before Leroy, also performed many of the chores dictated by a sharecropper's life. These two women learned hard work, and the values instilled by their parents. We knew the respect their father had for work: "I only missed three days of work in thirty years at the steel plant", their father, my grandfather, would boast, in his retirement years. I asked him, "you didn't ever get sick?' " Well, yes", he replied. "I would sometimes feel bad, but I would go on to work, because if you still worked in the field, you had to work sometimes feeling not so good."

As the oldest grand, I saw this hard work ethic, not only in Georgia and Josephine, but in the uncles as well. As I reflect on my growing up years, my mother, aunt, and uncles all worked long hours and, most times, several jobs, all at the same time. The "strong work ethic" is a value that is passed down in the Stover family and generations to this day. For example, I remember my mother working many Baylor Shifts (a creative, flexible shift that allows a nurse to work several hours at different locations simultaneously, to earn additional income) at the same time, and hearing about the Baylor Shift in the Nursing Profession from my aunt, also. Likewise, Uncle Leroy moonlighted to earn extra pay. Uncle Norman, the sixth sibling, a first in his own right, worked for the Max transit system in Birmingham, for years. He was the First Black President of the

Max Transit Union and retired in this position. Uncle Albert, the seventh sibling, is a retiree of forty years, from the Los Angeles, California City Civil Service, as well as the Post Office. He also exhibited the "strong work ethic".

Another important value passed from Uncle Leroy's parents was "putting something in your head"; in other words, getting an education. It is the key to your advancement in our society. No one can take that away from you, his mother, Bessie, would say. When the door opens, be ready to walk through it, was echoed constantly during the era of segregation, in our schools and homes. Uncle Leroy and his siblings grew up in this climate. I have often heard him say that you had to be" twice as good" as whites. I really think that this motivated him to constantly read, and push the bar to feel competent, in his own skin.

Uncle Leroy always had a strong disposition, was highly motivated, and appeared self-confident and unafraid. Because he was the oldest sibling at home, his father had high expectations of him in field work and assuming the responsibility of helping his mother. He loved his mother and the rest of us. In fact, he and his brother

Norman are still best buddies today. He drove us to town (Selma) weekly on Saturday, and to Church (Good Hope) on 4th Sunday. Uncle Leroy often bragged, "I could pick three rows of cotton at the same time and do a good job of it." I feel that he disliked or despised a lazy or lethargic person. He did not care for anyone who made a lot of excuses or was more negative than positive.

One of his early true life super-hero experiences, as a youth, occurred while chopping/hoeing cotton in the field. He decided to take a break, and go to the spring to get a cool drink of water. On his way to the spring, there was a sawed off tree top in his path. Sawmill workers had been harvesting trees in the area. Carrying his hoe with him, through this narrow path with tall grass on each side, Uncle Leroy decided to use his hoe and catapult himself over this tree top, being confident of his agile and sound athletic ability. When he landed in the clear area on the other side of this tree, there were thirteen rattle snakes of varied sizes lying in a circle, in the clearing, uncoiled. He immediately began to cut their heads off. He states that he worked fast before they knew what was happening. He showed this feat to his mother and his siblings. This confirmed to them that he was really strong, daring, and a remarkable young man. Uncle Leroy had to have nerves of steel to handle this frightening situation in his teens. Only God knew he would need this same stamina and tough disposition approximately seventeen years later, in Birmingham.

The Shiloh High School years were very busy for Uncle Leroy and exciting for me. I started the first grade at Five years old. He was a Junior in High school. This was a comprehensive school that had the first through 12th grades in several buildings.

Geneva, Leroy, Zettie Mae

I soon learned my role as an intercessor or go between message carrier. The young ladies daily sent messages to my uncles: "tell your uncle I said hello" was the most frequent message. I would have to describe the young ladies because many times I did not know their names, but my uncles themselves, had an idea who the person was or hoped it would be. Leroy was editor of the "Shiloh High News and Views".  Using his athletic prowess, Leroy participated in three sports, basketball, baseball, track and field. He still maintained a straight "A" average. He was Valedictorian of his Senior Class. He graduated May 16, 1952.

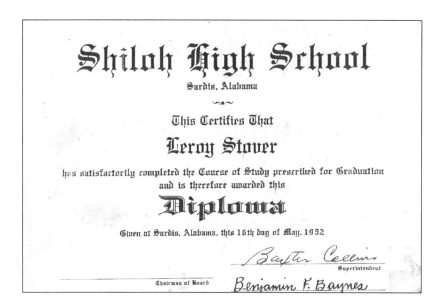

Uncle Leroy states that:

I received an academic/work study scholarship to Alabama State University through my Music teacher, an alumnus of Alabama State. But, after visiting the campus for orientation, I decided working in the kitchen just was not for me. From the field to the kitchen was not at all exciting.

Immediately after high school, Leroy joined the military, having signed on with the recruiter during

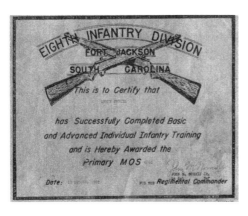

his senior year. He had a choice of any branch he wanted to enter. My Uncle was working in the cotton field the day before his birthday, when the recruiter came to pick him up. The recruiter parked his car in the yard and walked into the field where we were working and got permission from Leroy's mother for the enlistment. Uncle Leroy then went to the house cleaned himself and left with the recruiter. When my uncle left, my grandmother was so sad. As James and I played in our yard, we observed our grandmother would slowly walk around our house with her hands behind her back, looking down, praying, and humming. This made us sad, also.

Uncle Leroy successfully completed Basic and Advanced Individual Infantry Training, October 10, 1952, Fort Jackson, South Carolina. He was reassigned and completed The Infantry School at Fort Benning, Georgia,

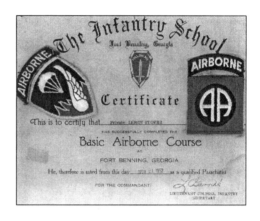

and was awarded the Basic Airborne Certificate November 21, 1952 as a qualified Parachutist. He was then reassigned to the Fort Bragg 82nd Airborne from November 1952 until Spring, 1953.

His assignment to the 187th Airborne Regimental Combat Team (RCT) in Korea began his overseas assignment, during the Korean War. After the Korean War ended in August 1953, his whole unit was relocated to Kyushu, Japan. I remember vividly receiving colorful satin Japanese jackets with the geography of the area on the back. Uncle Leroy sent me and my cousin, James, these beautiful jackets. When I wore the jacket to school, I had to stand in front of my class to let the other students see my jacket. My teacher obviously remembered my uncle and knew that it was from him in Japan (wow! that was such a big deal). Uncle Leroy remained in Japan until his discharge date in May 1955. He was discharged honorably.

During the next ten transitioning years, Uncle Leroy was an entrepreneur, salesman, fruit picker and poultry worker. During the summers of 1955 and 1956, Uncle Leroy, his youngest brother Albert and homeboys from Sardis went to Haynes City, Florida to pick oranges, tanger-ines, and grapefruits. He states that:

> The money was good approximately $125.00 per week. You could make the most from picking tangerines. But my skin became sensitive to the peach fuzz or leaves. In 1956, using the G.I. Bill, I attended Westfield High School Adult Education Trade Program in Upholstery. At one point I had dreams of possibly opening up my own business.

My uncle loves working with his hands. In fact, he is a natural mechanic. As long as I remember, my uncles could fix their automobiles. Likewise, restoring antique cars is a favorite hobby for my uncle today. He has a garage in his yard for this purpose. He has restored a 1985 convertible Eldorado Cadillac, as well as a 1988 Delta convertible Oldsmobile.

He began working for Progress Tailoring in Chicago, Illinois and sold tailor-made suits from 1956 – 1959, part-time. He measured, and sold suits to family and friends as well as the Ensley Jubilee Quartet Singers (a gospel group he sang with for ten years). He worked for Marshall Durbin Poultry for approximately three years, even after it moved from Birmingham to Jasper, Alabama.

To be closer to home and not travel daily to work, he began to work for Pratt Ensley Supply from 1959 until 1966. He was hired as a truck driver, but later also worked in the office in sales and measurement. It was his boss, Cordis Sorrell, who encouraged him to apply for a Policeman position in Birmingham. He even let him off from work for this purpose, and thought that Uncle Leroy would make a good policeman. Leroy states that, even when he did become the first Black Policeman, He would go and volunteer sometimes on his off days at Pratt Ensley

Supply. My uncle truly appreciated the encouragement from Mr. Sorrell, a Christian man, who helped change his life.

Part II

Birmingham Triumph: The Beginning

THE FIRST TEN YEARS (1966-1976)

Brannon J. Powell, B.A., MAT, ABD

A Historical Account

The Birmingham Daily News Paper read on
March 30, 1966
City hires first
Negro Policeman
Police Chief Jamie Moore
Today announced the hiring
of the first Birmingham Negro
Police officer and indicated
that a second will probably be
employed Thursday.
The first of his race to join the
Birmingham Police Department

Effective today, is Leroy Stover, 33, of 45 Ninth Avenue North. The second Negro who was certified by the Personnel Board as eligible for appointment as patrolman is Johnny Johnson. Chief Moore said in all probability Johnson will be hired, effective Thursday.

Another historical account:

Birmingham   Hires   First   Negro   Cop

BIRMINGHAM Ala APA has become the first of

his race to join the Department in Birmingham. He's Leroy Stover 33 a veteran of the Korean War who formerly was employed by Pratt Ensley Supply firm, said, "I could not describe my feelings of elation over the appointment." Police Chief Jamie Moore also said Wednesday that another Negro would probably be hired also. Civil rights groups have long protested the lack of Negroes on the Birmingham police force, page 17 NORTHWEST ARKANSAS TIMES, March 31, 1966: NewspaperARCHIVE.COM

It is clear from my Uncle Leroy as well as the many newspaper articles read that Kudos and homage should be paid to Chief Jamie Moore, who worked for the Birmingham Police Department as Chief from 1956 to 1972. According to the Birmingham Post Herald News Reporter, Daniel Connolly, Deputy Chief Stover remarked:

> Chief Jamie Moore took a special interest in me and Boswell (the 3rd Black police-man hired). He always encouraged and supported us. He checked on us daily. This was a usual routine for a supervisor, but unusual for a Chief of Police. Chief Moore supported us from the beginning secretly. He was more like a Dad looking out for us.

Coming on the heels of the Civil Rights Act of 1964 and the Voting Rights Act of 1965, 1966 was a tumultuous year. The following represents a Historical account of Birmingham, Alabama from many aspects, in1966.

In 1966, Springfield, Ohio had appointed the nation's first black Mayor of a smaller City and Birmingham, Alabama, the home of the Civil Rights Movement and staunch segregationist Bull Connor, hired its first Black Policeman, Leroy Stover.

> In 1969, a Birmingham News article, by Bill Mobley, stated that "Today, at 34, Leroy Stover lives in a far different world. He is the first member of his race to pass the Civil Service examination and become a Birmingham policeman." The article continues: "Officer Stover has been a credit to his race, or any race, according to Chief Jamie Moore. When a citizen recently stated, "Officer Stover is a good Negro policeman", Chief Moore retorted, "He is a good policeman, period."

Although the arrival of Officer Stover as a policeman was a sense of pride for himself, his family and the African American (then referred to as Negro) community at large. The early years often came with struggle and torment, even from his own community. The 1969 Birmingham News article observes;

> For the first few months as a Birmingham police officer, he was assigned to the Vice Squad as an undercover operative. He infiltrated illegal drinking places, card games and other activities that white policeman could not get into because of the color barrier.

Officer Stover then saw the other side of the big problem. In the article, Officer Leroy Stover is quoted as saying:

> They (other Negroes) got madder at me than the white policemen. I guess they thought I was just snitching on them and didn't really believe I was an officer.

This reference was in regard to illegal card games, gambling houses and bootlegging operations that Officer Stover had infiltrated. He then would call in white officers (as he was the only African American) to make the arrests. He said many Negroes were angry with him on many occasions. Also, Officer Stover noted that fellow

Blacks were not as cooperative with him in many cases as they were with white officers. He states:

> When I go to a big fight or other disturbances involving many Negroes, they expect me to listen to both sides of the story. Everybody tries to talk at the same time and many times I have to get really rude to shut them up. Most Negroes do not act like that to white officers.

> Although Stover encountered problems from fellow African Americans, this paled in comparison to the resistance faced from his white counterparts and society at large, at the time.

When speaking of his first day on the job, Officer Stover vividly remembers:

> I was brought in the roll-call room, and everybody moved to the other side. Being raised in the South under segregation, it didn't really phase me too much. I was accustomed to that sort of thing. That same day there were individuals (officers) who came up to me and said they would do everything they could to make

the transition easier. A few (officers) were nasty, but the majority were nice. I also heard the "N" word whispered but not to my face.

In a 2007 research unpublished manuscript by Charles Connerly, entitled "The Most Stubborn City In America: Birmingham, Alabama and the Integration of Its Police Department," it is stated that:

Stover traveled with two higher ranking policemen in an unmarked police car to the basement on the north end of City Hall where the roll-call for the North and South Birmingham precincts was then held. Stover and the two officers approached city hall from 19th Street North, where he recalls seeing a large, predominately white crowd gathered on both sides of the street. "Their reactions were mixed," Stover recounted, "I could discern the looks of hatred on some of their faces and I could see their mouths forming the "N" word as we drove past. There were others in the crowd who seemed to have a "wait and see what happens" expression on their faces.

The driver of the car sped up as they reached the inclined driveway that led underneath the north end of the building to an area called the "run-around" where most of the patrol units from the North and South precincts changed shifts. "I could still hear the noise from the crowd up on 19th and 20th streets as I was escorted down a long hallway that led to the roll-call room", said Stover.

My Uncle responds to this article:

After entering the building, my two escorts turned and went up a stairway that led to the first floor, I was alone then to walk about 20 paces down the long hallway by my self to roll call. I had already prayed, and felt that everything would be alright. As I got closer to the roll call room, several officers, looked up the hall-way and saw me, and began yelling, "Here comes a Nigger, and he's got on a police uniform and he's got a gun".

I'm thinking to myself, I'm going to have a problem, and I had better not make any sudden moves with my gun or anything like that. That was one reason, I thought it best to try and remain cool and calm, rather than nervous, jittery and making sudden moves. I continued walking into this large room and that's when they all moved to the other side of the room.

Stover continues to explain what you may not know from the article:

I was partnered with D. M. Alexander on the first day, but he drove off without me, leaving me in roll call without identifying himself. After roll call, I was still hearing negative remarks, pulling their guns and blowing imaginary smoke on the barrel. As officers moved out to the runaround to make relief, I followed them looking for my car and my partner, but neither one was there. I saw several cars but no number 63, my assigned unit. I stood there until all the units and officers were gone. I still stood there, hoping that car 63 would show up. When it didn't, I walked back to roll call room and three Sergeants were still sitting at the long table. The Lieutenant had gone to his office. When I walked in a certain Sergeant, yelled, "What the Hell are you doing still here?" I replied, "I am waiting on my relief unit and the officer that I am supposed to work with". He yelled, "Your unit does not make relief in the runaround. It makes relief at 3rd Avenue South", which was about three miles from the runaround. This Sergeant said, "If you don't get your Black Ass on over there, I will write you up for being AWOL, right now. I'll give you twenty minutes to get there." I said, "How am I going to get there when my car is at the Police Academy". The Sergeant replied, "Ain't that too damn bad". I just stood and looked at him. He would not look me in the eye and went back doing his paper work. I went on back out to the runaround saying to my-self, I have got to get on over there some kind of way. As I approached the 19th street exit, I was thinking I will catch me a bus. When

I exited on 19th street, the crowd began to yell "there's that colored Policeman, Where is He going?" Some said, Those low down SOB's, they are sending him back home. I started walking on across 19th street on the west side of the street. Most whites were on the east side near city hall, the Blacks were on the west side where the Greyhound bus station is located. As I approached the bus stop in the middle of the block, several younger ladies yelled, 'He sure is cute", several older ladies were heard saying, "I prayed for colored Police". They all surrounded me.

In about two minutes, I saw a Birmingham Transit Bus, come across 8th avenue and pulled up to the Bus stop. I waited until the ladies got on the Bus, and that's when the Bus driver saw me (He is white), and yelled "Hey, you are that colored policeman". I was still a little hot under the collar, I yelled back, "yes, I'm that colored policeman". He said, "I don't mean any harm, where you going?" I replied, "I am going to my beat". He said, "Where is that?" I replied, "They told me 3rd avenue and 35th street south". He said, "Come on, get in", so I did.

I stood on the upper step next to the driver. (Remember, Black people were still riding on the back of the bus). The front section was filled with mostly mature white ladies, and the back section mostly filled with Colored ladies. There was an empty row of seats between where the whites were sitting and the Colored passengers began. I observed that these seats were reserved for more whites. The Colored passengers passed these seats and continued to fill up the back seats.

The driver conversed with me and said, "you mean those low down SOB's would not take you to your beat?". He explained to me that his bus was not the one for my address I had given him. His route was 6th avenue south and Titusville. I had seen that on the Marquee, when he pulled into the bus stop. But, I took the first bus that came along. As we approached first avenue north, the bus driver told me, "what the Hell, I'm going to take you to your beat, they'll just have to fire me." So, when we approached 3rd Avenue South, he turned east on 3rd Avenue toward the location of my beat. Riders on the bus replied, "Where is He going?" The driver replied, "Ladies, I'm going to take this Officer to his beat". This was the first time someone had respected me as an Officer, from the other race. He said, if any of you want to get off, I'm coming right back this way, and I'll pick you up then. No one made an attempt to get off, but they turned red in the face and made no further comment.

When we arrived on 35th street, unit 63, I observed, was parked under a tree, with a white officer behind the wheel. The bus driver pulled into the parking area and as I exited the bus, the colored ladies said again, "I'll be praying for you, and you be careful out there, for it's some low down white folks out there", I replied, "I thank you". In my excitement, I thanked the bus driver, but forgot to get his name. The Bus driver also told me "you be careful now". *The bus driver was a God send just for me at this time.*

As I waved to those on the bus along with the bus driver, I approached unit 63, the passenger window was down and I looked in and spoke to the white officer, sitting behind the wheel, with the motor running. He did not say a word. I opened the passenger door and placed my night stick between the cushion and upright back seat. I placed my left foot on the floor of the car, and in the process of sitting down is when this white officer jerked the car in gear, and took off, that caused me to abruptly sit in the seat with my right foot still on the outside. The sudden forward motion caused the open passenger door to slam shut. I had to jerk my foot up quickly, to keep from getting hurt. The force still struck my shoe, but I was not injured. I immediately said, "You fool, you could have hurt somebody". He replied, "If you can't stand the heat, get out of the kitchen". I tried to make small conversation, but He would not say a word.

Everywhere we went, the beat was all white. We got our first call, he picked up the mike, I picked up the clip board to write, He immediately slammed on the brakes, throwing me against the dash board, and snatched the clipboard from my hand. And made the comment, "ain't no damn Nigger going to put his hands on my clipboard". I said, "I thought everything in this car was city property, including the clipboard". But I did not try to take the clipboard back, because that would have probably started a fight, which they would have wanted. I just kept my cool. (Thank God). The Dispatch in fact called us back just to make sure everything was alright, because of the time delay in responding to the call. He told the dispatch, everything is 10 - 4. When we arrived at the call destination, it was all white folk, they were looking at me, and crowded around the police car. I got out the car and stood outside in order to back my partner up, if needed. They were asking questions to Alexander about me, "They put that Nigger with you today?" Alexander replied, "yea, but he ain't going to last long". I saw him coming back and got in the car before he got to the door.

We proceeded on the beat to the next call, many people were waving and I waved back. Alexander would turn red, but would not say anything. We got the second call, I was bracing myself with my other hand, as I reached for the clipboard. He slammed on the brakes, and snatched the clipboard out of my hand. I just looked at him and laughed. He wrote down the pertinent information and placed the clipboard back in its place. We arrived on the scene, just as the first call, white people crowded around the police car mostly out of curiosity. There was no hostility from those around the car, only the partner in the car. He replied again to those who ask about me, "he ain't, going to last long", is what Alexander told the crowd. He completed the paperwork on that call. We started patrolling again, and received the third call. We went through the same procedure as before, He picked up the mike, snatched the clipboard away; I just really laughed. It is the same ritual as before. This ritual began to get old, really. On the fourth call, I fooled him, I pretended to pick up the clip board, but I didn't, he assumed I had the clipboard, reached for it; I told him wrong place. I started laughing at him, He turned beet red. Reluctantly, reached down on the seat and got the clipboard.

The rest of the calls were uneventful, I didn't try to take the clipboard. I just really waved at the crowd on the rest of the calls. I did exit the car as I should and stood as back up if needed until lunch time. At about mid shift, I asked him doesn't this car have a time to eat lunch and a place on the beat where you can eat. (I had seen in the roll car room on the bulletin board). His reply was, "yea, but I don't stop to eat". I later learned that, the senior person dictates, what goes on in the car and has control of the car. You can complain to your supervisor, but you cannot tell the senior Officer how to run the beat.

Alexander and I worked on for at least another hour, this is now about 8 O'clock on the 3pm to 11pm shift. He got so hungry he stopped at a small service station on his beat on 5th avenue south and Crestwood Blvd. operated by a white male. He proceeded inside talking to the operator of the station, while both were looking out at me. He got some change from the operator. Then, he went to two vending machines outside the station, proceeded to get cookies and a soda and went back inside where the operator was. I was hungry too, so I proceeded inside the station to get change for a dollar. He looked at Alexander and then proceeded to give me the change for a dollar. I went outside and got me some crackers and a soda. I stood by the car and proceeded to eat my snack. I could hear him say again, "He ain't going to last long".

After this we proceeded to patrol until quitting time. About ten minutes till 11:00, he pulled back to the relief point. He got out of the car, got his brief case and night stick, went to his private car and drove off. I was still sitting in the police car, he never said a word. I sat in the car for about ten minutes, when two cars drove up. These two police officers parked their private cars and walked up to this unit car 63. They said, "Good evening Officer, Good to see you, Where is Officer Alexander?" I said "he is gone, as you can see, he left me here". They then said, "Where is your car?" It's at the police academy, they took me to roll call", I replied. "You mean he did not take you back to your car?" I said, "no". These officers then began to berate Alexander for his actions. These officers said, "He is one of the worse police officers we have, they put you with him in order to *run you off"*. These nice Officers said, "It is off of our beat but we are going to take you to your car". They in fact took me to my car at the police academy. I thanked them and they said, "I will see you again tomorrow". They figured that I would be assigned with him again the next day. These events ended my first day on the job.

My Uncle Leroy reflects on day two at the Birmingham Police Department:

On the morning of day two, prior to going to roll call, I went to a store and bought me an inexpensive brief case. Then I went over to my mother's house and asked her to fix me a lunch. I was going to be prepared that day and ahead of Alexander, in case he did not stop for lunch again. My Mama could smother some pork chops. She fixed me pork chops and fried chicken and those hot baked biscuits that she made and I loved. She wrapped all of this in waxed paper and placed it in a brown paper bag. So after I ate at my mother's house, I had to go and get ready for my shift, which began at 2:30 p.m. I drove my own car to roll call this time, and the scenario was the same as the day before, when I entered roll call room, All the other officers moved to the other side, while making the same derogatory remarks, such as "the nigger is back"; the only time that it was quiet was when the assignments were being called out, as the Sergeant yelled "Listen up for roll call". At no time did these superior officers make an attempt to stop the antics and name calling.

Sure enough my name was called out for car 63 and working with Officer Alexander this second day. As the day before, he never held his hand up or acknowledged his name, but he didn't have to because I recognized him on the other side of the room, from having worked with him the first day. After roll call, all officers exited to the run around to make relief. I made a quick exit to my personal car that was parked on 20th street, knowing that I had to drive up to 3rd Avenue and 35th street south. I drove to the assigned area and beat Alexander there, and signed for the car before Alexander arrived. I was in the unit car 63 sitting down on the passenger side when he arrived. He approached the car and got in behind the wheel. I spoke to him but he did not say anything. It was the silent treatment again. He just drove off, and we starting patrolling. On this day, we received several calls, but I let him do all the work. He would answer the mike, then, stop the car and write down the information, then put the clipboard back in place before we took off again. This went on all evening until about mid-shift. When people saw our car, they would come out and wave at us; when we arrived at the call destination, he would still tell people the same thing " Yea, They put him with me again but he ain't going to last long". About mid-shift I asked him, "Are we going to eat?" He replied, "NO", we ain't going to eat. I later learned that the place assigned on the beat to eat was a white establishment, and he did not want to take me there.

Unknown to Alexander, I had placed my brief case on the back seat with my lunch in it of chicken and pork chops. I got my lunch bag out and opened it. The delicious aroma filled the air. He turned red as a beet. The first thing I opened was a pork chop and started eating. He drove on as fast as he could while still beet red, as I munched on my delicious pork chop. As I finished, I tossed the bone out the window, because there was no anti-littering law on the books. So we drove on, answered a call or two. Later on, he got so hungry and stopped by the same little service station as the day before. As he pulled up to this station, I said, "I thought you weren't going to eat anything", He again got so red, and went on into the station.

While, he was in the station, I got out of the unit car, placed my bag on the trunk and finished eating the rest of my lunch.

Both of them were again talking and looking out at me. This day, I brought my own change, and went to the soda machine and got my own soda. He got his customary cookies and soda and stayed inside talking to the operator. After I finished eating, I was going to wash my hands, so I went to the door of the station and asked the operator, "Is there a restroom on the side of the building"? He did not say anything, but looked at Alexander, and both of them just stared at me. So, I just turned and went on around on the side of the building where the restroom was located. Above the door, there was a sign that read "Whites Only", I tried the door, it was unlocked, so I went on in and used the facility. I came out, got my brown lunch bag off of the car, put it in the trash can, then I went and sat on the passenger side of the Police Car. He stayed in there talking a long time, he came out when he heard a call coming in on the radio. We responded to that call and didn't receive any more calls that night. When shift changing time came, it was the same scenario as the day before. He got his night stick, his brief case, left the car, got in his personal car and did not say a word. I got out of the Patrol Car and waited for the relief shift to show up (you cannot leave your vehicle alone). The same two young officers showed up. They said, "They were glad to see that I survived, and they won't put you with him anymore".

As my uncle was telling me his story, I wondered, if these young officers had complained to their superior officers and the word got back to Chief Moore. My uncle stated that "whatever, the case, I was not assigned with Alexander anymore". He was assigned on the third day with a more liberal Officer; "He was more equitable in his views with regard to Blacks and Minorities. I knew that because of the way that he interacted and treated me. His name is E. K. Martin."

On March 3, 1969, Uncle Leroy was admitted to the University of Alabama (UAB), College of General Studies, Birmingham, Alabama as an undergraduate student. This quest continued on a part-time basis until his completion.

This decade presented many challenges in Leroy Stover's life. He continued his quest for education at the University of Alabama (Birmingham). He completed the Bachelor's Degree in Criminal Justice in June, 1976.

Many of his certificates, training, and accomplishments during this period include:

Certification of Graduation	Birmingham Police Academy, 1966
Certification of Graduation	U.S. Civil Defense Corp, 1966
Certificate of Police Management	Law Enforcement Officer Training school, 1968
Police Instructional Methods	University of Alabama Birmingham, Fall 1970
Mayor's Youth Council	City of Birmingham, 1970
Certificate Handling Juvenile Offenders	University of Alabama Birmingham, 1970
Police Athletic Team	Birmingham Police Department, 1971
Theory and Operation of Intoximeter	Alabama Police Academy, March 26,

1971

Police-Community Relations Award	Samford University, August, 19, 1971
Training in Supervisory Techniques	University of Alabama Birmingham, Fall 1972
HONORARY CITIZEN	City of Kansas City, Missouri, July, 14 1974
B.A. Criminal Justice	University of Alabama Birmingham, June 6, 1976

My uncle reflects on his transitions during this time span:

In 1972, I was promoted to Sergeant and worked as a Detective. I investigated any crime that took place except homicide, which had a specialized unit. Later, I also worked as a Patrol Supervisor at one of my favorite precincts, the West Precinct, for about a year. Then, I was transferred into Internal Affairs for about seven years, until my promotion to Lieutenant. At this point, I was transferred to the West Precinct, as a shift supervisor on the 11:00 p.m. to 7:00 a.m. shift. I was in this position for about two years.

PART III

The Second Decade

1977 – 1987

Minita Powell-Clark – B.A., M.A.T., Ed. S.

1977 to 1987 was a time of transition for Leroy Stover. In this decade he held various positions and earned his stripes. Additionally, this time period also represented many important things culturally, socially and politically.

In 1982, Stover was promoted to lieutenant. He held this position from 1982-1984 at the Westside precinct on the 11 to 7 shift. From 1985 to 1986 he was lieutenant on the South side on the 3 to 11 evening shift. In 1987 Stover moved to the East precinct. During this decade, lieutenant Stover was moved around with a purpose. He distinctly remembers the precinct commander telling him that he is to "straighten out the shifts". As Stover recalls this decade of his career he uses the term "troubleshooting" to describe much of what he did in this decade. When Stover, Birmingham first black policeman, would go to different precincts he was considered a shift commander. This meant that he was in control of approximately 40 to 50 police officers. He also supervised 4-5 sergeants who each had his/her own set of officers that reported to them. As a shift commander, Stover reported directly to the precinct commander. In this role, the shift commander is to keep the precinct commander abreast of the daily goings on of the department either orally or in writing.

The shift commander was still an important position. The precinct commander only worked the day shift, 7-3. So for the remaining 16 hours of the day, on the remaining two shifts, from 3 to 11 and 11 to 7, the shift commander was the top cop on duty.

At this point race relations amongst Sergeant Stover and his peers was less of a problem than in the previous decade. By this time, Stover had been on the police force since 1966 (nearly eleven years) and had earned a reputation for being "firm and fair". His even handed demeanor helped to smooth things. Additionally, Stover had the power of the pen and said that, "his other officers respected authority and his position".

However, the road to climbing the hierarchical ladder was not always easy. Sergeant Stover was interviewed in the *Birmingham News on December 18, 1980. He was asked by Birmingham Times Reporter, Franklin Tate, "Why no black lieutenants, captains or deputy chiefs*?" Stover responded:

> Because of the way the promotional system is set up, the chances of a black being promoted above sergeant are very slim. He also adds Birmingham's system gives one point to an officer for every year on the force and inherently that discriminates against blacks whether intentional or not.

In this aspect, Sergeant Stover is speaking historically and referencing the fact that blacks traditionally have not been on the force as long as their white counterparts and are often times excised before they accrue any years, as evidenced by this quote from the same Birmingham News article in December of 1980:

> Numbers of blacks have been discharged because they supposedly didn't communicate with other officers. Some was said not

to be aggressive enough or doesn't take initiative.

My uncle recalls that:

During this period, approximately fifteen Blacks were dismissed during these struggling years, usually during their first year, when they had no recourse. For years the total number of Blacks on the Birmingham Police force remained less than ten.

Leroy Stover was never promoted on the consent decree, because he always scored high enough on the test, usually #2 or #3. He provides these comments for explanation:

For example, there were eleven lieutenant slots available, three blacks were promoted to lieutenant from that list. One person was # 19, the other # 27, but all three Blacks were promoted because of the Federal Consent Decree. In fact, this opened up the opportunity for Blacks hired after me in all positions to be promoted.

A federal consent decree is defined as a final, binding, judgment for a voluntary agreement between parties (essentially a settlement). Once entered, a consent decree is binding and cannot be reviewed except on showing that the consent was obtained by fraud or that the decree was based on failure of consent. A typical consent degree usually agrees to cease certain illegal conduct or behavior and consents to a court to barring such conduct in the future (in this case discrimination).

My uncle reflects further on the consent decree:

> This Federal consent caused a backlash among white police officers, because of the practice of passing over so-called more qualified white officers who were higher up on the roster, to promote a Black officer to an open slot for a particular position. These white officers would call those promoted under consent decree "welfare officers". But, in fact, they respected those who scored high enough to get promoted on their own merits. The hostility became more subtle, over the years.

Uncle Leroy has been in the Birmingham Police Department for at least fourteen years. During this tenure, Sergeant Stover has confronted many issues including racism, bigotry, and promotion within the Police Department. In a *Birmingham Times* newspaper article, written on December, 18 – 20, 1980, by Franklin Tate, it states that, *"Sergeants Stover and Johnson discussed that they were not bitter about what they had encountered."* On November 20, 1987, Stover was promoted from Lieutenant to Captain. He is congratulated by Mayor Richard Arrington, First Black Mayor of Birmingham, and former Dean at Miles College of the Co-editor, Dr. Don L. Powell, Miles Honor graduate, 1967.

Mayor Richard Arrington congratulates Lt. Stover on
promotion to Captain

Precinct Captains: Stover, Cochran, Walker, Webb

Birmingham Post-Herald +

■ Movies C2
■ Deaths C3
■ Classified C4

METRO

Deputy chief finds

By Steve Joynt
Post-Herald Reporter

Cordis Sorrell pulled one of his truck drivers aside and gave him a little advice: Become a police officer, he said.

The truck driver, Leroy Stover, thought it sounded like the right job for him, but the problem was that Birmingham didn't have any black police officers.

And not because blacks weren't interested in the job.

"Several blacks had passed the test by then, including a professor from Miles College, but the city always found reasons to not hire

civil rights activist pushing for me. That apparently made me a little easier for them to take."

On March 30, 1966, Stover was hired as Birmingham's first black police officer. One day later, Johnnie Johnson Jr. was hired as the second.

This week, Johnson, who became Birmingham's first black acting police chief only four months ago, promoted Stover to the rank of deputy chief.

Sorrell, though, wasn't around to see it. Stover's former boss died a little more than a year ago.

"He always followed Leroy's career and all of his promotions," said Sorrell's widow, Mildred Sorrell. "My husband was very proud of Leroy, and he felt like he had a little bit to do with making history by talking Leroy into taking the police exam."

A black Ensley businessman and an active member of Jehovah's Witnesses, Sorrell believed he had a civic

Pastor O.C. Oden and Deputy Chief Stover

Chief Johnson and Deputy Chief Stover

Awards – Promotion Ceremonies

Awards – Promotion Ceremonies

Awards – Promotion Ceremonies

Captain Betty Gamble (first Black female officer) and
Mother congratulated by Deputy Chief Stover

Mrs. W. Herring, precinct Secretary, Captain Trucks

Candice, (Granddaughter) graduation from Spelman College- Oprah Winfrey was the main speaker (Spring, 2011)

Oldest Daughter Juslyn at Jaymesen (high school gradu-ation, Modesto, Ca,) and Jechia (Leroy's grandchildren)

City of Birmingham

RESOLUTION

WHEREAS, the Council of the City of Birmingham is proud to join the Metropolitan National Association for the Advancement of Colored People in honoring their 1998 Outstanding African Americans; and

WHEREAS, these honorees have made invaluable contributions in the fields of Education, Religion, Business, law Enforcement, and Community involvement, and

WHEREAS, the 1998 Outstanding African American Honorees are:

Dr. Geraldine Bell, Former Superintendent Birmingham Public Schools
Children Workshop, Grassroots Youth Action Organization
Mrs. Sharron A. Daniel, Community Affairs Officer, Colonial Bank
Mrs. Lillie M.H. Fincher, President Top Ladies of Distinction
Mrs. Edna Miller Gardner, Owner Smith & Gaston Funeral Services
Councilman Aldrich Gunn, President Pro-Tem Birmingham City Council
Mr. Calvin Haynes, Community Leader
Chief Johnnie Johnson, First Black Police Chief for Birmingham, Alabama
Reverend Awalski Moore, Youth Pastor New Hope Baptist Church
Dr. Albert Sloan, II, President Miles College
Deputy Chief Leroy Stover, First Black Police Officer
Dr. Perry Ward, President Lawson State Community College
Miss Tyreinda Williams, 1997 America's Junior Miss
Reverend/Dr. Bernard Williams, Pastor Mt. Moriah Baptist Church
Mr. Willie Young, Legend in Negro Baseball

NOW, THEREFORE, BE IT RESOLVED by the Council of the City of Birmingham, with Mayor Richard Arrington, Jr. concurring, that we hereby commend and congratulate the 1998 Metro Birmingham NAACP Outstanding African-American Honorees.

RESENTED this Twenty-Seventh day of February, Nineteen Hundred and Ninety-Eight by Council President William A. Bell.

PRESIDENT OF THE CITY COUNCIL

COUNCILMEMBER

COUNCILMEMBER

COUNCILMEMBER

COUNCILMEMBER

COUNCILMEMBER

COUNCILMEMBER

COUNCILMEMBER

MAYOR

ATTEST:

CITY CLERK

City of Birmingham

RESOLUTION

WHEREAS, the Council of the City of Birmingham would like to recognize Leroy Stover, the first Black Birmingham Police Officer who joined the force on March 30, 1966; and

WHEREAS, Leroy Stover attended Shiloh High School in Sardis, Alabama and obtained a Bachelor of Science Degree in Criminal Justice from the University of Alabama in Birmingham; and

WHEREAS, Leroy Stover joined the U.S. Army in 1952, and in 1955, he received an honorable discharge; in 1991, he was appointed Deputy Chief of the Birmingham Police Department; and

WHEREAS, Deputy Chief Stover has served in many capacities since employed as a Law Enforcement Officer; five years as a Police Officer, and was one of the first of two Tactical Officers, ten years as a Police Sergeant; over five years as a Police Lieutenant; over five years as a Police Captain, and five years ago was appointed Deputy Chief; and

WHEREAS, Deputy Chief Stover currently serves as Chairman of the Board of Deacons at the Antioch Baptist Church in Fairfield, Alabama; member of the Mayor's Community Relations Committee; member of the Northern Area Chamber of Commerce; member of the Northern Area Block Watch Association; a charter member of the Birmingham Guardians Association and member of the National Organization of Black Law Enforcement Executives (NOBLE).

NOW, THEREFORE, BE IT RESOLVED by the Council of the City of Birmingham, with the Mayor concurring, that we hereby commend and congratulate Deputy Chief Leroy Stover for 30 years of loyal and dedicated service to the Birmingham Police Department and this City.

BE IT FURTHER RESOLVED that he receives this Resolution as a token of our sincere gratitude for his courageous efforts to serve and protect the citizens of this City.

ADOPTED unanimously this Fifth day of November, Nineteen Hundred and Ninety-Six.

PRESIDENT OF THE CITY COUNCIL

COUNCILMEMBER

COUNCILMEMBER

COUNCILMEMBER

COUNCILMEMBER

COUNCILMEMBER

COUNCILMEMBER

COUNCILMEMBER

MAYOR

ATTEST:

CITY CLERK

Metro Birmingham NAACP branch salutes outstanding African Americans

The Metro Birmingham branch of the NAACP held their annual "African-American History Celebration" saluting outstanding African Americans Feb. 27, at the historic Sixteenth Street Baptist Church. The program is held annually as a tribute to African Americans who have made accomplishments and achievements in the Birmingham area. The 1998 honorees included Dr. Geraldine Bell, Sharron A. Daniel, Lillie M. Fincher, Edna Miller Gardner, Councilman Aldrich Gunn, Calvin Haynes, Johnnie Johnson, Awalski Moore, Dr. Albert Sloan II, Leroy Stover, Perry Ward, Tyrenda Williams, Rev. Bernard Williams and Willie Young.

sful
ning
local

were
'ugh
ocal
nt of
er of
Jean

nnae
their
ding
s for

Part IV

The Third Decade

1988 -1998

Bessie Stover Powell, B.S., M.A., Ed D.

In 1988, Stover remained Captain until 1991. His first assignment as Captain was Commander of the West Precinct, for about two years, until 1990. The Birmingham News reported in an article by staff Writer Roy Williams on October 19, 1990, *Police shake –up all part of plan says deputy chief, Charles Newfield* that, administrative changes within the Birmingham Police Department during the past few months were made to provide a new look and feel to the force. One of the New Commanders was Captain Leroy Stover, West Precinct, he was switched from the East Precinct. In 1990, Stover continued the fight to rebuild community crime watch groups and help combat the ongoing crime issues in area neighborhoods. He petitioned them to be "nosy and on the lookout" for strange behaviors. Community residents expressed their concerns openly and with hope of weeding out the "trouble spots" with police assistance. Overall, they were pleased with police response in the area but did note that sometimes it takes longer than expected for an officer to arrive once called. Stover noted that the department was facing a shortage in officers and that because their area spans such an enormous radius, it can take one who is on duty several minutes to arrive at the location of the new call. He provided the residents a sense of comfort in knowing that their communities can be safe, but that a unified

Police shake-up all part of plan, deputy chief says

By **Roy Williams**
News staff writer

Administrative changes within the Birmingham Police Department the past few months were made to provide a new look and feel to the force, Deputy Chief Charles Newfield said.

All four of the department's precincts, along with such offices as homicide, narcotics, robbery and auto theft, have new leaders.

Newfield said the changes were not a spur-of-the-moment decision, but an established plan to help improve the department's performance.

"These changes have been made over the last three months, not all at once," Newfield said.

"It's a sound administrative move to look at your organization and change it from time to time. It will give commanders an opportunity to view different areas of the city and help in their career development."

The new precinct commanders are:

● Capt. Bill Gaut, North Precinct. Gaut was commander of the East Precinct.

● Capt. June Webb, East Precinct. Capt. Webb was administrative assistant to Newfield.

● Capt. Leroy Stover, West Precinct. Stover was switched from the East Precinct.

● Capt. Eugene Mosby, South Precinct. Mosby is a former commander of the West Precinct.

The department's homicide office is now headed by a former homicide detective, Lt. Robert Walker. Walker, a former lieutenant in the north precinct, took the place of Lt. Chuck Jordan, who now oversees the robbery division.

Former robbery Lt. Teresa Thorne was transferred to a supervisory position in patrol.

In addition, Capt. Julius Walker switched from the Police Academy to oversee narcotics and vice. The new head of narcotics is Lt. James Hope. Former narcotics Lt. Bob Berry is now a supervisor of patrol in the East Precinct.

Julius Walker, who began his new job eight weeks ago, said his main goal "is to make a dent in the drug problem in Birmingham" through initiative must remain in tact. He later was transferred to North Precinct, allegedly to "straighten out the precinct."

During this time, my uncle worked in an environment where the population of Birmingham was around 265,000 people, according to the Census Bureau. Also, in the 1988-1998 ten year time - span, several important events impacted the financial environment of Birmingham, Alabama. The city has become prominent for the medical facilities and treatment through the University of Alabama at Birmingham. The Birmingham area was known as the "little Pittsburgh of the South", as well as the *Heart of Dixie* (symbols of racism and segregation). The Mercedes Benz plant opened in 1994, in Vance-Tuscaloosa, Alabama.

Johnson promotes first black officer to deputy chief

By Roy Williams
News staff writer

Johnnie Johnson, Birmingham's first black police chief, has promoted the city's first black police officer to the rank of deputy chief.

Leroy Stover, formerly commander of the West Precinct, started his new position as deputy chief in charge of patrol on Thursday.

Stover, 57, was the first black to join the force when he was hired March 30, 1966. Johnson, who became acting police chief in August, joined the Birmingham police department one day after Stover.

Stover becomes the department's second black deputy police chief. The other is Deputy Chief John Fisher, who heads the tactical division and police academy.

Johnson, a former deputy chief, has not filled the fourth deputy chief slot.

Stover takes over a position formerly held by Deputy Chief Charles Newfield, who recently replaced the retired Howard Miller as head of the detective division.

As deputy chief of patrol, Stover will oversee the department's four precincts and all other uniformed officers working at various substations. He said his biggest goals are to "cut down Birmingham's drug problem and violent crime in general."

Stover said the public holds the key to winning the crime fight. "We need more public awareness in what their responsibilities are," he said.

Stover credited much of his success to the late Cordis Sorrell, a white Ensley businessman who encouraged him to quit his job as a truck driver and apply for the police force in 1966.

"He talked me into taking the (police) exam," Stover said. "What I've accomplished can show black officers that if they obey rules and regulations and study hard, the opportunities (for advancement) are there."

The plant rolled its first ML Mercedes SUV off its assembly line in 1997, a positive impact for the economic enhancement to the city of Birmingham area.

In 1991 Leroy Stover was promoted to Deputy Chief. In this article, written by Roy Williams, *Birmingham News* staff writer (2-8-1991), entitled, "Johnson promotes first black officer to deputy chief" it states that:

> Johnnie Johnson, Birmingham first Black police chief, has promoted the city's first black police officer to the rank of deputy chief. Leroy Stover, formerly commander of the West Precinct, started his new position as deputy chief in charge of patrol on Thursday. Stover, 57, was the first black to join the force when he was hired March 30, 1966. Johnson, who became acting police chief in August, joined the Birmingham police department one day after Stover. Stover becomes the department's second black deputy chief. The other is Deputy Chief John Fisher, who heads the tactical division

and police academy. Stover takes over a position formerly held by Deputy Chief Charles Newfield, who recently replaced the retired Howard Miller as head of the detective division.

The article further states that:

As deputy chief of patrol, Stover will oversee the department's four precincts and all other uniformed officers working at various substations. Stover said his biggest goals are to "cut down Birmingham's drug problem and violent crime in general". He said that the public holds the key to winning the crime fight. We need more public awareness in what their responsibilities are.

My uncle encourages others in this article, stating that:

What I've accomplished can show black officers that if they obey rules and regulations and study hard the opportunities (for advancement) are there.

During this decade, Uncle Leroy participated in the Birmingham Police Gospel Choir. This effort was originally formed at the request of acting Chief Johnnie Johnson, who requested some officers get together to sing carols at the Ketona Nursing Home. The group liked singing

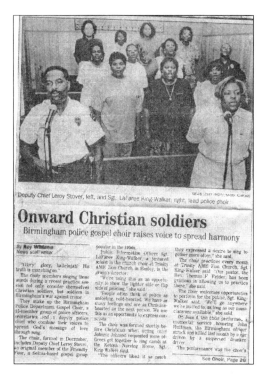

Deputy Chief Leroy Stover, left, and Sgt. LaFaree King-Walker, right, lead police choir

Onward Christian soldiers
Birmingham police gospel choir raises voice to spread harmony

together so much that they expressed a desire to continue, and welcomed opportunities to perform within the community. Deputy Chief Stover had performed in quartets since a teenager. He still leads songs, in the Male Chorus and Gospel Choir, at the Antioch Baptist Church, Fairfield, Alabama.

While commenting on his tenure, my uncle states the following:

> When you are a deputy Chief you can make policy, specifically over those that I was responsible for, which was Field Operations (uniform division). One of these

programs was *Bicycle Patrol.* The *Bicycle Patrol* was used to supplement the patrol units, particularly downtown, in shopping centers and parks. This helped to have a higher visibility in these areas. I utilized males and females, Black and White. Some of my best bicycle officers were females.

Deputy Chief Stover describes another program instituted:

> I also instituted the *Walk and Talk* program. The beat officer would park their patrol unit and walk certain areas to get to personally know the residents. This was an effort to help the relationship between the police and community; because in the past, people would only see the officer when something happens, make an arrest, write the report and leave. But the *Walk and Talk* program was to help ease tensions as well as help the officers to know who lived on their beat. This way the people in the community had a vested interest in the police department because they felt that the police had their welfare as a priority.

Another program Stover instituted was:

> The *Better City Services Sergeant Program.* This program entailed citizens calling in complaints directly to their precincts, about issues in their neighborhood. These issues could be overgrown lots, no lights on streets, pot holes in the

street, vacant run down houses, water running in the street and any other quality of life issues. This came about when I would visit the Neighborhood meetings. Citizens would often complain to me that they would call these various city services and get no response; therefore, I told the citizens to call these complaints into their various precincts. We would relay these complaints to the various city agencies directly responsible, such as the water, gas, lights, sewage, and the parks and recreation departments who could help clear up these matters. These matters would be relayed to a Sergeant at these precincts. As a result, these problems were solved expeditiously, when the police department called the needed department. At subsequent meeting, citizens reported that these problems were in fact being handled in a timely manner.

Another program Stover instituted was:

The *Good Morning Card Program.* In this program, cards were printed for officers with their names (ID) on them, and particularly the night shift officer, as they checked the businesses on their beat, they would leave this card to let the business owner know that they have checked their facility. The time the business was checked was indicated on the card. They were left in the door of the business. These cards were also used to check the elderly citizen on their beat who might live alone. The time was also indicated when the premises were checked.

One of the last programs that Deputy Chief Stover instituted was:

A *"Language Program"*. This program was instituted during the 1990's when there was an influx of Spanish citizens in the Birmingham area. The purpose was to help the officers to enhance their communication skills in basic Spanish, so that officers could communicate with Hispanic citizens on their beat. Most Hispanics would use the term "no comprende" when questioned by officers (even if they understood, many were limited English proficient). At that time there were only two officers who were known to speak Spanish in the department. Therefore, when a Hispanic needed to be questioned or information concerning their constitutional rights provided, we had to use these officers to communicate with them. Therefore, I ordered Spanish training materials including books and tapes for each precinct. Specific instructions were given to be used during roll call training. The training information was basic, with such phrases as what is your name, where are you going, where are you coming from, do you have a weapon, and even included "put your hands up"; in other words, common language used by an officer but in Spanish.

My favorite initiative, states Chief Stover, was:

The "HICOPP" - High Intensity community oriented Police Patrol. This unit was made up of officers from the various precincts that have shown great potential in their police work and had been proven to make critical effective decisions on their own. They were utilized to target hot spots in the city, primarily in the housing units, and inner-city communities for high crime areas. Their primary purpose was to saturate these areas with high visibility. To neutralize or eradicate any crime that existed. They worked as a team - a single unit, and when crime was neutralized, they were moved to other targeted areas without the general public knowledge. The aim was to target these areas without the criminal's knowledge of their where-abouts. This proved to be very effective in these areas and bolstered the confidence of the public with the police in these areas.

During my tenure, overall crime was reduced about 15%, other than homi-cide, which the police have less control over. The police through high visibil-ity can reduce robbery, assaults, auto thefts, burglaries, but have less effect on homicide. All the programs instituted by me seemed to be very helpful to the offi-cers in performing their duties, as well as the community, during my tenure. I believe that most of these programs that

I instituted still exist, in some form, in the Birmingham Police Department.

I surmise that my uncle believed in high professional growth and development for his officers. He wanted his officers to think smartly, and be safe on the streets. In an article from the Birmingham News, February 1, 1995 entitled, *Deputy Chief: Lone officer often at risk*, Stover talks about the risks of an officer working alone:

Two police officers are better than one when it comes to handling confrontation with groups of people, especially in high crime areas. Usually people are less apt to jump on police if there is more than one officer. With two officers, you can neutralize a situation before you have to resort to deadly force.

He further states:

I strongly believed in physical fitness for my officers, states, Uncle Leroy. I led as an example for these officers. In my 65th year which was my retirement year, I still scored around 100 on my physical fitness test.

In the Birmingham News article, written by Walter Bryant, entitled, *City's First Black Policeman retires,* it states that*:*

Deputy Chief Leroy Stover, right, laughs with the man who followed him onto the police force, former Police Chief Johnnie Johnson.

City's first black policeman retires

By Walter Bryant
News staff writer

In 1966, Leroy Stover was looking for a better way to provide for his family when he became the first black to join the Birmingham Police Department.

But by wearing a badge for 32 years and reaching the rank of deputy chief, he became a symbol for other officers and a pioneer in breaking the department's color barrier. He retired Friday.

"I was driving a truck for a Pratt City construction company, and my boss encouraged me to apply to be a police officer," Stover recalled. "I told him that I worked 5½ days a week, and couldn't get off to go take the test."

His boss gave him the time off to apply and on March 30, 1966, Stover reported to work for the first time in a police uniform.

At his Friday afternoon retirement party, Stover recalled that he had to be escorted by superior officers into City Hall for roll call at the start of his shift.

He said growing up in rural Dallas County prepared him for the racism he encountered at first. And his combat experience as an 82nd Airborne Division paratrooper dur-

ing the Korean War taught him to carry out orders.

"It just didn't faze me," he said of the initial racism he met. "It rolled off my back."

The white officer he was assigned to ride with in a South Precinct car accepted him as an officer, but not as a person, he said.

"That first day, we took care of police business, but we didn't talk," Stover recalled.

He said at the beginning of his career he only wanted to be a good officer, and rising through the ranks was not a dream.

"But after I made sergeant, my aspirations raised a little," Stover said. "And when I made lieutenant, it raised a little more."

Stover said he has received one job offer, but he has no set plans for his retirement years other than coming more active in his church, Antioch Baptist in Fairfield.

Retired Birmingham Police Chief Jamie Moore, who was chief from 1956 until 1972 and hired Stover, said he set the tone for Stover's eventual acceptance.

"I let it be known on the department, that we were going to abide by the law," he said.

See **Retires**, Page 8A

Deputy Chief John Fisher, in charge of training said, Stover has continued to set an example of physical fitness. He scores 98 or 99 on the Fit Check, an annual physical fitness exam officers have to pass.

My uncle called the Police Payroll (Human Services Department) in order to ascertain the number of minorities, as well as the total number of officers in the Police Department. He states the following:

There are 832 total officers. Out of that number there are 391 black males and 107 Black Female police officers. To date, there is a total of 498 Black police officers on the force. This represents a total of over 60% of officers on the police force who are Black. This is compared to 000000000.1 of 1% back in 1966, when I first started on the police force.

During the 1998 year that my uncle retired, it was noted in The *Birmingham Post Herald* article, by Lewis Kamb, *First black police officer retiring*, that Blacks make up 471 of the 888 officers in the Birmingham Police Department. I questioned my uncle about the decrease in the numbers of over-all Blacks, and he responded as follows:

> This could be reflective of the demographic shift (white flight) to the more affluent suburbs. Suburbs such as Shelby County, Hueytown, Pelham, Pinson, Hoover, Mt. Brook and Vestavia, were all glad to get experienced trained officers from the Birmingham Police Department. It saved these cities the cost of training these officers. As a result, the Birmingham Police populous would always fluctuate, because of the lure of other cities offering higher salaries to experienced officers. In recent years, there has been a shift of whites returning to the inner city in loft style condominiums or apartments, in the downtown vicinity. I feel that this return is to help them regain their political clout within the city of Birmingham. Presently, there are predominately Black elected officials within the city government.

Many of Deputy Chief Stover's training and accomplishments during this decade include:

1. Award- Northern Block-Watch and the Northern Neighborhood Association for EXTRAORDINARY LEADERSHIP AS PRECINCT COMMANDER, 1989

2. Outstanding Achievement Award - Birmingham Guardians Assoc. 11-23-90

3. Public Safety/Law Enforcement, The City of Birmingham, Office of the Mayor, 09 -20 - 1991

4. Domestic Violence Seminar - Birmingham Police Academy 02-26-1992

5. Scroll of Appreciation – Birmingham Community Schools, The Advisory Council of Project S.O.A.R., 1992

6. Executive Management Seminar, U.S. Department of Justice, Federal Bureau of Investigation, April 14-16, 1992

7. Certificate of Appreciation, Participation of the Youth Day Program, The Youth Department of First Baptist Church Airport, 07-14-1992

8. Certificate of Appreciation- Birmingham Urban League Summer Youth Work Education Enrichment Program, The Birmingham Urban League, Inc., 08-07-1992

9. Honorary Staff of the Attorney General of the State of Alabama, State of Alabama, Jimmy Evans, Attorney General, 08- 24, 1992

10. Certificate for Participation and Completion of the Southeastern Law Enforcement Executive Development Seminar, FBI, 10-1992

11. Certificate of Commendation –Perfect Attendance, Office of The Mayor Birmingham, Alabama, 11-20-1994

12. Certificate of Training: "Violent Crime: Using Law Enforcement Resources More Effectively", spon-sored by the Law Enforcement Coordinating

Committee- Northern District of Alabama, 05 – 4-6, 1994

13. Service in Police Community Relations working with underprivileged children in the P.A.T. Police Athlete Program for over 12 years

14. Member of the Mayor's Community Relations

15. Member of the Northern Area Chamber of Commerce.

16. Member of the Northern Area Block Watch Association

17. Charter Member of the Birmingham Guardians Association

18. Member of the National Organization of Black Law Enforcement Executives. (N.O.B.L.E)

19. Member of Metro-Birmingham Branch NAACP

20. Award –Birmingham Emancipation Association NAACP Service Award, 1994.

21. Special Recognition Award- U.S. Marshall's Office for Heading Police Security for OPERATION OLYMPUS-Olympic Games in Birmingham, 1996

22. Award Resolution –City of Birmingham for 30 years of loyal and dedicated service to the Birmingham Police Department and the City.- 11-5-1996

23. Award- Outstanding African American for 1998 - NAACP, Birmingham, Al.

My uncle had earned the respect of many of his fellow officers as well as in the community. As I reflect on the significant role of my uncle, it was evident in the funeral procession of his mother. Given the segregationist history of the south in general, Birmingham and Selma in particular, It was unbelievable to see all the police cars and motor cycle uniform officers, many white, riding in front of our motorcade. There were five family cars along with the hearse. We had not seen this picture before except for a president or royalty. But here we are in Birmingham, (the seat of racism), Scott McPherson Funeral Home is carrying my grandmother, Uncle Leroy's mother back to Selma Alabama, across the Edmond Pettis Bridge, the scene of the historic Selma to Montgomery March, and we are led by several police cars driven by an integrated police force. It is doubtful that many people had seen, or experienced this before. As we went through small towns, the local police would have on their lights, out of respect to this large funeral motorcade of police passing through. I asked my uncle what was his response to seeing all the honor and respect shown him at his Mother's illness and Home-going (Funeral) Celebration, in January, 1997; his response:

> It was really a humbling and gratifying experience for me to see the respect and love that was shown me and my family during this time. I feel that, it was the result of the fairness and respect that I

tried to exhibit from the beginning which seemed to be pouring out on me, at this time of grief and bereavement. Words are inadequate to explain how I really felt. It seemed to be approximately, twenty-five cars and sixty-five to seventy-five uniformed officers that went to Sardis, Alabama, over 100 miles away to support me as their Commander. In the beginning, all the White Officers isolated and rejected me, but in the end, we all came together as one, displaying love, admiration and respect. This indicated to me the impact that I had on their lives for over 31 years.

As I went to the front of the church, to give the remarks at my grandmother's (uncle Leroy's mother) home-going for the family, I was almost in awe, as I looked to the back of the church, and saw all the White and Black Uniformed Officers, at my grandmother's services, because of her son, their Commander. Rev. Ward, Pastor of the Church, and Dr. McPherson, Pastor and Funeral Director, also acknowledged Chief Johnson and the Birmingham Police Department. I reflected on how unusual this situation is. My grandmother had to be special, to have two sons that were first, in Birmingham, Alabama. Leroy is the first Black Policeman, and Norman is the first Black President of Max Transit Union. Yet, all of us were back at our roots, in rural Sardis, Alabama, where we were sharecroppers at a different point in time.

As I reflected on the historical significance, as I crossed the Edmond Pettis Bridge that I had crossed weekly as a little girl, I remembered many family members that lived in the Selmont Community, on the right. As the motorcade turned off of Highway 80, onto Highway 41, I remembered that my Uncle Leroy had taken my cousin and me to the Old Drive-In Theater many times during the summer. I only knew that we sat on the car hood to watch the big screen. It was only as an adult that he was reflecting that Blacks were not allowed to go to the movies and other facilities. I questioned him and learned when he said that:

> The Black teens would drive in the back
> of the Drive-In behind a white fence, and
> they would ask someone (White) to turn
> up the speakers, on the back row.

I must admit that as a seven year old, I never saw the fence that divided the Black and White race.

When I asked my uncle about the picture of him and President Clinton, he responded:

One of the high lights of my career was when the President of the United States, President Bill Clinton, visited Birmingham Southern University. Several Presidents had visited the city during my tenure, but at the time I was just on security detail and never that close, but only secured their motorcade as they passed on the city streets. But with President Clinton, it was different, I was In charge of security while he visited the city. When he finished his speech, and moved outside

to shake hands with the public, I went along with the President as he proceeded to shake hands with the public. There was a fence that separated the public from the President. He would lean over the fence to shake hands and in order to keep him safe and from losing his balance or falling as he leaned over to shake hands, I would hold him by his belt. Secret Service was behind me and all around, but I was right next to the President and holding him by his belt. He went along the fence for over 100 yards, shaking hands over this fence. That is because he was such a popular and people oriented president. When the hand shaking session was over, secret service escorted him back inside the building. I stayed outside to help manage the crowd. But, the President sent for me, I learned later that the President had asked Chief Johnson, who I was. He wanted to take a picture with me. When I went inside the building, President Clinton, with his White House Press Photographer, took pictures with Chief Johnson, and me. President

Clinton thanked me for the excellent job that I was doing with security. He asked me my name and rank and I told him. He said I'm going to autograph a picture and send it to you. I said, "I appreciate that Mr. President, and Thank-you". At that time, I shook his hand and went back to my duties. Chief Johnson stayed with the President and his detail.

Stover further states that:

I didn't think too much about it, I really didn't think that the busy President would take the time out to autograph a picture and actually send it back to me, because I realize that the President takes pictures all the time, with various individuals. But to my surprise, about two weeks later, a large brown manila envelope was delivered to my office, addressed to me, with a return address from the President of the United States. I could hardly wait to open it; when I did, it was an autographed picture from the President of the United States, which read "To Deputy Chief Leroy Stover, Best Wishes", signed Bill Clinton. I have had a lot of good things that happened over my lifetime, but I would have to say that this is the most exciting and memorable.

Joe Ann (wife), Stover, Lisa (daughter)

My uncle has always been people oriented; he reflects further that:

I want to thank my staff especially during my tenure as deputy chief. Because of their professionalism and hard work they always made me shine. Thanks go out to my secretary, Mrs. Henrietta, Pat, and Glenda. My various assistants over that time, Roy Williams, and Crutchfield, who left after a short time, and my right hand man and staunch supporter, Captain Charlie Trucks. Captain Trucks is a good guy, a *real* policeman, and a *real* person. He is a good friend, who later became a Chief of Police in Homewood, Alabama.

There was an outpouring of love, support, and respect for Deputy Chief Stover at his retirement in 1998. According to *The Birmingham News,* in an article written by Walter Bryant, entitled, *City's first black policeman retires,* Accolades poured from colleagues as they recalled Deputy Chief Stover's influence on their lives and careers for 32 years. He was described as a trail blazer, by Chief Johnnie Johnson, who further states that:

Stover and I stuck together in the early days. "We were like a lump of coal in the middle of a white sheet". We had to play off each other for moral support in order to endure the kind of things we did in those days". "This is the end of an era," he said. "We went from the bottom of the totem pole to the top, together."

Retired Chief Jamie Moore, said, "I let it be known in the department that we were going to abide by the law"; Homewood Police Chief, Charles Trucks, even stated that Stover's participation as a para-trooper in wartime earned him a "silent respect" from his white counterparts, even from the beginning. Chief Trucks was on the Birmingham Police Department when Stover joined in 1966. Stover, in response to the overwhelming approval and praise from all over, simply responded by saying that "it was God that put me in the position to be the first black police officer. We have a good department and you all have been a blessing to me."

Part V

Family Reflections

Minita Powell - Clark, B.A., M.A.T., Ed. S.

All of the responses are composed from personal interviews with Uncle Leroy's family members. Several responses are in question and answer format.

Josephine Wallace – (Sister, Birmingham, Al)

Minita: Tell me about your, and Uncle Leroy, and other siblings upbringing and the kind of home in which you were reared.

Josephine: Well our parents were very strict. They were tough. They taught us to be honest and treat everybody right. We were all very cooperative with each other as siblings and were kind and loving.

Minita: I bet that contributed to some of Uncle Leroy's "stickler" habits. What qualities did he have as a young child:

Josephine: I remember that he always did his best to accomplish any task that was given him. Of course you know he still remains that way today.

Minita: I can believe that. What was his personality like as he grew older (in his teens and early twenties) that would lend itself to those of a law enforcement officer?

Josephine: He was a strong personality and kind of demanding at times. He was still a very nice person but he would demand that each person played his part in anything where he was involved. He didn't like when people goofed off and wanted them to be an effective team member. On the job I'm sure he was the same way.

Minita: Clearly he was and those qualities only intensified. Most people don't lose what has been ingrained in them over a long period of time. You mentioned Uncle Leroy accomplishing anything he set out to do. What do you think was the highlight of his career?

Josephine: Him accomplishing rank after rank and continuing to climb the ladder all the way to reach the title of Deputy Chief was something unheard of back then. That was great; that was his highlight.

Minita: Yes, that is phenomenal. And to do it all with such high regard and respect for people and from people is what really makes the accomplishment stand out. Do you think his religious beliefs played a role in the way he conducted himself as an officer?

Josephine: Oh yes. He was a devout church member and Christian so that gave him the assurance that when he went out on the job that Jesus was with him and protecting him everyday. We were brought up in the church and we didn't have a choice to not go.

Joe Ann Stover – wife

I called Joe Ann on a Wednesday evening around 7:15 p.m. It had been quite awhile since we had spoken and she told me it was good to hear my voice. I, too, informed her that I was equally as pleased to hear hers. We made a bit more small talk and I proceeded to ask her if I could quickly interview her about my uncle, and her husband, Leroy. She said, "Oh sure, I was in the kitchen but go right ahead". I thanked her and told her that the questions I'd be asking were centered on their meeting and her observations and perceptions of him as a notable officer in the Birmingham area.

Minita: So first let me start by asking how long have you known Uncle Leroy?

Joe Ann: Oh wow! (she laughs) I've known him for nearly 40 years. We've been married since 1991. July 20, 1991…that's 22 years.

Minita: That's a long time! I didn't realize you had known him far before you had gotten married. How did you meet?

Joe Ann: Well Leroy was working at the Police Department and I worked for a store called Loveman's Department Store downtown. You know how the officers check on businesses. So he would frequently stop through.

Minita: Ok. And how did you perceive him at that time?

Joe Ann: I could tell that he was an honest guy who always strove to help people that were down.

I could tell that just in his conversation. If he felt someone needed a helping hand or even some words of encouragement, Leroy was the one to give it. He would even try and talk sense into the criminals. He'd tell them that there was a better way and that they didn't have to commit crimes to have a better life. And he wouldn't be yelling or in a rage, he would just very calmly give advice… to anyone male or female.

Minita: That's great. Was he the same way at home? Or would you see a "different" Leroy?

Joe Ann: (Laughs) Well, you know, if there was a bad night at work or something (and this was infrequent and during the early part of our marriage) he would come home with a "police attitude". I would just have to tell him "lower your tone, Leroy. I'm not the secretary or a criminal". And I would tell him that I'm your wife, but most of all I'm your friend. So we got over that hurdle rather quickly. I was kind of no-nonsense myself so it didn't take long for us to get an understanding (we both laugh).

Minita: I understand (chuckle). He had to learn how to separate the two and he did. So tell me what was Leroy the "Officer", "Lieutenant" and "Deputy Chief" like in your opinion?

Joe Ann: He was strict; very neat and clean. His pants were always pressed with a deep crease. He always kept himself in tip top shape and even though he had a big belt and gun, he looked good! (we both laugh again). It was his mannerisms that really caught my attention though. He was always, always professional. He showed that he respected people and would even say "yes ma'am" and "no sir."

Minita: Seems like he had the personal and professional lives in tip top shape. What would you say about his relationship with God? I know he is a devout Christian and church goer.

Joe Ann: Yes. A key point in our relationship was that Leroy loved the Lord. He teaches Sunday school and he is over the Deacons Ministry. He puts God first, and then me. He sings in the choir and he is a man of God. Humble.

Minita: Yes. That is definitely him. Well, my last question is does Uncle Leroy have any special quotes or sayings or Bible verses that he lives by? That people may often hear him say?

Joe Ann: (thinks to herself). Yes. If you hadn't of asked that question I would've never thought of it like that. I noticed that years ago when someone (anyone) would ask him "How are you?", He would say "oh, I'm blessed". But the last several years, whenever anyone says, "How are you, Leroy?", he'll say "I'm better than I deserve." That speaks volumes.

Norman Stover – (Brother, Best friend, Birmingham, Al)

Q. Tell me about your, Leroy and other siblings upbringing and the kind of home in which you were reared.

> We were raised in a strict Christian home. We had rules to follow and if rules were broken, we were punished. All the siblings got along well together. Leroy and I got along very well, even until today we are not only brothers but best friends.

Q. What is the advantage of this?

> You know each other, your strengths and weaknesses, likes and dislikes which helps you to be a better friend.

Q. Describe Leroy. (Your best friend)

He's a well mannered person. He is quick thinking, very generous, and would give you the shirt off his back. He is well mannered, but don't push him too far.

Q. How do you think this helped prepare him to be the first Black policeman in Birmingham?

He has no fear. He is willing to try anything. Being a paratrooper in the Military helped him. Jumping out of planes also helped him to be able to conquer his situation.

Q. Reflect back, How did you feel when Leroy went to the Military, since you all were still in rural Sardis?

I was devastated when he left to go to the military. I became closer with my younger brother (Albert).

Q. What were you thinking when Leroy became the First Black Policeman in Birmingham?

He would share all of his thoughts with me and how he was treated. He told me how they sneaked him through the back door on his first day.

Q. What made him endure these first days on the Job with the Birmingham Police Department?

He was a strong willed person. He didn't think that anything or anyone could defeat him. He had a strong faith in God and a praying mother. So, faith and prayers played a big part in his success and tenure at the Birmingham Police Department.

Georgia Stover Ramsey – (Oldest sister, Orangeburg, SC)

Q .Tell me about your, Leroy and other siblings upbringing and the kind of home in which you were reared.

We had lovely parents. They were strict. They taught us to always love one another, and our church. We had to go to Sunday school every Sunday. We walked to Mt. Olive No.1. They taught us hard work in the home and the field. They taught us a high work ethic.

Q. Tell me about your relationship with Leroy.

My relationship with my brother is very good. I am about six to seven years older than Leroy.

Q. Are there any special qualities of your brother, Leroy?

Yes, he is courageous. He has always been strong. Because, I remember the time that he killed all those rattle snakes, and he was a teenager. He chopped their heads off. He was quick thinking.

Q. Your thoughts upon hearing him become a policeman.

I was living in Cleveland, Ohio at the time. I was happy when he became a policeman, I knew he would make a good one, he was strong, didn't get too excited. I believed he could handle it.

Uncle Brother – youngest brother

My grand uncle, in Los Angeles, California, nicknamed "Uncle Brother" is Uncle Leroy's youngest brother. He was more than happy to give me information on Uncle Leroy as a big brother and as the brother who became the first black police-man in Birmingham, Alabama.

Minita: Hey Uncle Brother.

Uncle Brother: Hey there. I'm ready to answer your questions (chuckles).

Minita: Well alright, let's get started then. I've already spoken to both your sisters and they gave me the background on Uncle Leroy as a young child. What can you tell me about him in school...growing up?

Uncle Brother: Man, in school, nothing bothered or fazed him. All the girls loved him but he wouldn't pay then any attention. A crowd would even follow him around the school. He wouldn't pay any mind to anyone. He was all about getting his books.

Minita: Wow. He was that smart...and obviously handsome.

Uncle Brother: Oh yea. Leroy's ways were much different than anyone of us. We might be hanging out somewhere and he would just go home. He liked familiar stuff and he was always the same.

He was a straight "A" student and he put his all into everything he did.

Minita: What about in his spare time? What kind of activities did he engage in?

Uncle Brother: Well he was very athletic and good in sports. All my brothers and I sang in a quartet as we were growing up. Leroy was good at that. He would be the lead most of the times. And we had to go to church *every* Sunday; most of the time that meant walking 4 or 6 miles to get there.

Minita: Now that's a lot to take in. He was a great student, athlete and singer. That's outstanding. So did it surprise you at all when he decided to become an officer? When did he tell you?

Uncle Brother: No it didn't surprise me at all. You see, being in the military gave him experience at keeping order and settling conflicts and things like that. So no, I wasn't surprised at all. I first heard it on the news that Leroy was the first black police officer. I was already here in Los Angeles at the time. So then I called to Birmingham to talk to the family.

Minita: How did that make you feel (to know that your brother was the first black policeman)?

Uncle Brother: I felt proud. Anyone should be proud of their siblings that are doing something positive. It made me feel real good. I always knew that he would do anything he put his mind to.

Minita: I keep hearing that he accomplished anything he put his mind to from each one of his siblings and I think that is just amazing. Not many people can say that anything they set their minds to gets accomplished; never deterred.

Albert C. Stover – Youngest Brother (follow-up Q and A)

Q. Tell me about your, Leroy and other siblings upbringing and the kind of home in which you were reared.

> We had strict rules, be polite to people, respect the elders. We had to follow those rules in the home and out of the home.

Q. How do you think this helped Leroy?

> I feel that these strict rules helped us all to carry through and do whatever task we had

to do. You had to do whatever needed to be done, whether you liked it or not

Q. How would you describe Leroy?

He acted different. He wouldn't say much, just go on and do what he had to do, in other words, just get the job done. He liked reading. He would read detective books.

Q. How did that difference work for him?

He just did what he had to do. We were taught not to be bullies and to ignore the negative things.

Q. What were your thoughts when hearing he was the first Black Policeman in Birmingham?

My wife's family members heard it on the News in Los Angeles, California. We were very concerned about his safety.

Donald Edward Ramsey (Leroy's Nephew, Sacramento, California)

Q. How old were you when Uncle Leroy became the first Black Policeman?

I was ten and a half years old, and living with my grandmother, (his mother) when my uncle became the first black policeman. I thought it was a major achievement. I was proud of a Black man wearing the uniform, and he was always immaculate. I had never seen a Black man in a police uniform before. He was representing our family, our city and our state of Alabama.

Q. Did anyone ever discuss this with you?

I recalled a young lady came up to me in my class at Englewood Elementary School and ask me about it, and told me how proud she was to see my uncle as a Black man and in our family, and the first Black Policeman in Birmingham, She was just as proud as I was.

Q. As a ten year old did his disposition change to you?

No, he never changed from before he became a policeman, and during the time he was a policeman, and during his retirement , his disposition is the same, someone that I can go and talk to, even now.

Q. Is there anything else you want to reflect about your Uncle?

He is a very kind man. He would go out of his way to help anyone, regardless of their race, creed or gender. This is something that I know personally. I remember the time when Uncle Leroy wanted me to be a policeman, but I felt bad when I said no, because I felt I was not ready to wear a gun on my side, or to represent the city of Birmingham. I felt that I had let him down, he reminded me of how good I was with numbers and knowing the city. But later in the Military, I did become a shore patrolman. Uncle Leroy is the one who got me into traveling. Between the ages of eleven and eighteen, I had traveled to California with him at least three times. During the times he came to Ohio, I would also travel with him to visit family.

Q. Some family members say that your personality is somewhat like Leroy's. What kind of Uncle was he to you?

He was closer to me like a father figure, friend, teacher, and mentor. He is not one to sit around and wait for something to happen. He makes it happen. If there is a task at hand, he gets it done. It is an honor and a privilege to be thought of like him. I was living with my Uncle Leroy when I married my wife Deborah, over thirty three years ago.

Dr. James Wallace (oldest nephew, Barnesville, Ga.)

Q. Tell me about your earliest recollection of your uncle as well as your relationship with him.

When I first knew that He was my mother's brother, my uncle and also my friend, a good friend to me, he always respected me, and a good friend of a life-time. One of my earliest recollections is when he taught me to drive. He sat me on his lap and trusted me to steer the car. My feet could just reach the foot pedal. He trusted me enough to let me drive his car as a sixteen year old to my Senior Prom. Through the years, he has been a friend, given me good advice and that has been through the years. Early on, I perceived him as a good friend to others, who always had friends, I remember that he and several of his friends got together to give one of them a needed bath. I remember that they chased him all through the field. From this I believe that Uncle Leroy just wanted this person to be more socially acceptable. They were teenagers at the time. This goes to the heart of him trying to help a person to be better and do better. That is the kind of person he is.

Q. What qualities do you feel he possessed that helped him during his tenure?

Foremost, His belief in God. That God is his protector, and leader. He knows that Jesus Christ is our Savior. Truth, faith and hope when obviously under stress, and he had to believe that God was leading him through his valley experience. Even in our valley experience God is working in and through us. What I've seen in his life is a Christ – like spirit, trying to help people, trying to be beneficial and concerned about people. I think that his whole tenure at the Birmingham Police Department was wrapped up in his faith.

Q. During 1966, you were a junior at Case Western Reserve University, Cleveland, Ohio, what were your recollections when you came home to Birmingham during the summer.

When I went home, I saw Uncle Leroy in the uniform and I was proud. He showed me his equipment and shared some of the events going on, some good and some not so good. We always talked over the years. I was extremely proud of him. He wanted to move up from patrolman, to higher positions. He had the drive and intelligence to achieve these goals. He has always had a sense of humor, not necessarily jokes. But Uncle Leroy and I have a communication between us that we laugh about even until today, called *Skulker. Skulker* is a crusader against crime in the comics. Leroy would call himself that. It is about crooks and villains, and one who is always fighting crime. This is a continuous joke every time we see each other, we get a good laugh.

Q. What are your thoughts about the Funeral and Home-going Services at his mother's passing with all the Birmingham Policemen present.

Considering the whole picture, a Black family having all the authority of the Birmingham Police Department at their services is amazing. Another thought just came to me of how proud my grandmother (his mother) was to see him accomplish and reach that height in the Birmingham Police Department. Of course, I am still extremely proud, even in his retirement.

PART VI

Summary

The saga of Leroy Stover, Birmingham Alabama's first black policeman is one of repeated triumphs against overwhelming odds. This is the ingredient that makes his notable life such an inspirational story. It begins in the grueling and desolate cotton fields of rural Sardis, Alabama, where Leroy learned strong and vigorous daily work ethic that would sustain him throughout his illustrious career as a police officer. We follow Deputy Chief Stover from his early high school days at Shiloh High School, in Sardis, Alabama, to his triumphant career in Birmingham, Alabama. We see early leadership skills and intelligence on the part of the young Leroy as he becomes editor of his high school newspaper. A notable high school record as vale-dictorian and athlete would be followed later by a stellar stint in the U.S. Army, as a paratrooper, in the 187th Airborne Regimental Combat Team (Korea/ Japan). Courage, character, strength, and determination marked Deputy Chief Stover's amazing military career.

The strength and fortitude exemplified by Deputy Chief Stover as a paratrooper would serve him well as he broke the color barrier to become Birmingham, Alabama's first black policeman. It must be remembered that this deep southern city had acquired the reputation of being one of the most rigidly segregated in the country. Eugene "Bull" Conner, Birmingham's arch-segregationist and Police Commissioner, reigned. He ordered dogs to attack peaceful marchers in 1963. The atmosphere was therefore rife with discord, bitterness, racial hatred, and intolerance. It is against this oppressive backdrop that Leroy Stover would eventually emerge as Birmingham's first black policeman on March 30, 1966. However, his journey, while thoroughly inspiring, would not be easy. He encountered repeated opposition from most of the white police officers on the force, deliberate attempts on their part to prevent him from doing his duty, and had constant racial epithets hurled at him. A lesser man might have folded under such intense pressure and scrutiny. But as we have seen in this narrative, the resilient character of Deputy Chief Stover was formed early on in life, obstacles and barriers were only challenges and risks to be taken and conquered. His commendable service and bravery as an 82nd paratrooper in the U.S. Army, made a universally admired quality. He eventually won over many of the entrenched segregationist white officers on the Birmingham police force. They silently respected his military service and courage. The reader comes to see that it is the combination of these qualities, and perhaps others, such as firmness and fairness, that would eventually catapult Leroy to the rank of Deputy Chief on the Birmingham police force.

His story, however, would be incomplete without acknowledging the whites of good will who helped to make Leroy's ascension possible. Foremost among these was Chief Jamie Moore who was Chief of Police in Birmingham from 1956 to 1972. Stover has always acknowledged that Chief Moore took a special interest in me and Boswell (third black hired), like a dad. Cordis Sorrell, who was

Leroy's supervisor at the Ensley – Pratt Building Supply Company, also played a pivotal role in Leroy's life by encouraging him to take the test and apply for a position on the Birmingham police force – going as far as to let him off, to do so.

The family reflections included in this book are meant to help authenticate the true story of Deputy Chief Stover. They represent the intimate and revealing observations of his accomplishments, personality, and overall character as recounted first by the author, his oldest niece, nephews, and siblings. Further insight into the inspiring story of Leroy is provided by the many newspaper clippings and articles that are included in this book. Collectively, along with Leroy's own words and reflections, they represent the actual accounts of his remarkable breakthrough as Birmingham's first black policeman, his rise to power and respect, not only in Birmingham but also throughout the nation. This is dramatically borne out in the picture showing Leroy shaking hands with then President Bill Clinton, on the latter's visit to Birmingham Southern University in 1998. Leroy played a key role in escorting the President during the visit. Other pictorials highlight various aspects of Deputy Chief Stover's exceptional career. Another picture shows Leroy being congratulated as he is promoted to Captain by Mayor Richard Arrington, who served as Birmingham's first black mayor for several terms. Overall, this book is dedicated to Leroy's triumphant and inspiring life. The man who was once denied access to a position on the Birmingham police force rose through the ranks, to become the Deputy Chief of Police with over 800 on the force. He treated all under his command firmly, fairly, and equitably. This is the legacy of Deputy Chief Leroy Stover, who has earned his place in history.

Bibliography

Bryant, Walter. *"City's First Black Policeman Retires,"* The Birmingham News 1998

Connerly, Charles. *The Most Stubborn City in America: Birmingham, Alabama and the Integration of it's Police Department. Unpublished Research, April 9, 2007.*

Gavin Floyd, Shirley, *Leroy Stover First Black City Policeman Birmingham, Alabama. The Foot Soldier Informer, October- January, 2003. Vol. 1.*

Joynt, Steve. *"Police choir shows different side of job".* The Birmingham News 10 October, 1992. Sec. E3

Kamb, Lewis. "First black police officer retiring" Birmingham Post-Herald 04-1998. Vol. 131 no. 223.

Northwest Arkansas Times, 31 March, 1966. NewspaperArchive.com

Tate, Franklin. *First Black Policemen Not Bitter.* The Birmingham Times, 18-20, December 1980.

The Birmingham Daily News Paper, *City Hires first Negro Policeman. 30, March 1966.*

Williams, Roy. " Johnson promotes first black officer to deputy chief" Birmingham News 08 -02- 1991.

CPSIA information can be obtained at www.ICGtesting.com
Printed in the USA
BVOW011612060613

322647BV00001B/1/P

9 781625 097156